BLUFF YOUR WAY
IN
MUSIC

PETER GAMMOND

RAVETTE BOOKS

Published by Ravette Books Limited
Egmont House
8 Clifford Street
London W1X 1RB
(071) 734 0221

First printed 1985
Reprinted 1987, 1988
Revised 1991
Reprinted 1992
Revised 1993
Reprinted 1994

Series Editor – Anne Tauté

Cover design – Jim Wire
Printing & binding – Cox & Wyman Ltd.
Production – Oval Projects Ltd.

The Bluffer's Guides® is a
Registered Trademark.

The Bluffer's Guides series is based
on an original idea by Peter Wolfe.

An Oval Project
for Ravette Books Ltd.

CONTENTS

The Gentle Art   6

Order of Precedence   8
  Impresarios   8
  Agents   9
  The B.B.C.   9
  Recording Companies   10
  Conductors   12
  Virtuosos   14
    Singers   14
    Pianists   16
    Organists   17
    Violinists   18
  Musicians   19
  Critics   20

Composers   23
  Beethoven   23
  Mozart   25
  Bach   28

Other Composers (*see overleaf*)   29

Modern Music   48

A Few Musical Byways   50
  Music-Hall Songs   50
  Folk Music   51
  Light Music   53
  Jazz   54

Instrumental Odds and Ends   21
Conversation Piece   22

Glossary   55

Other Composers:

Bartók	29
Berlioz	30
Brahms	30
Britten	31
Bruch	32
Bruckner	33
Chopin	34
Debussy	35
Delius	35
Dvořák	36
Elgar	36
Grieg	37
Handel	38
Haydn	38
Liszt	39
Mahler	40
Mendelssohn	41
Rachmaninov	41
Schoenberg	42
Schubert	43
Strauss, Johann	44
Strauss, Richard	44
Stravinsky	45
Tchaikovsky	46
Tippett	46
Vivaldi	47

INTRODUCTION

If we took an average cross-section of the public (and, after all, the greater percentage of the public is cross most of the time about something or other), we would certainly find that at least 98 per cent of them (the other 2 per cent being deaf or convicted) were forced to listen to music in some form or other for at least 25 per cent of their wakeful lives. Only 4½ per cent of the 98 per cent really want to know about the technicalities of music or are interested in its murky and involved history.

This book is not written with the surreptitious intention of making you acquire a vast knowledge of music. Quite the opposite. The way to get on in life, as all good bluffers know, is to have a minimum of knowledge and make it go a long way by means of obscure words and profound pauses. Nor is it written, as most musical journalism is, for other critics and experts. They know all the tricks of the trade already and will not need any help from us.

To be at ease with a vast and complicated subject like music it is not necessary to know all the dates and all the theory (although there is nothing against knowing them if you feel that way inclined) but rather to appear to be on easy terms with the subject – to know what goes on in the backrooms, to cover your embarrassing enthusiasm with contempt, and to know the jargon.

This book goes quietly behind music and, in the nicest possible way, stabs it in the back. Absorb its querulous message and you will have taken the first steps away from being an innocent and rather nice dilettante and towards being a nasty but entirely successful bluffer.

THE GENTLE ART

Music, as we all know, is an indiscriminate mixture of melody, harmony and rhythm which most people enjoy in one or other of its many forms. Apparently most animals like it too, except dogs.

Its chief value is as a harmless drug. People in a more advanced form of world-weariness use pills, drink, cigarettes, money and religion to shut the general nastiness of life out of their battered minds for a time. Music has a similar effect and hurts no-one.

Only a very small percentage of the music we hear is played by professional gentlemen in tail-coats in large concert halls. Most of it is pouring out of radios, television sets, record-players and cunningly hidden speakers. Housewives, facing the appalling sordidness of the weekly wash, are encouraged to go on living by smooth gentlemen who play records for them; teenagers work off their pent-up dislike of their elders by playing primitive music at a terrific volume; motorists stop themselves from going mad in traffic-jams by listening to anything that happens to be on the radio at the time; diners in expensive restaurants are made able to face up to the bad food and the large bill by soft music percolating through the ceiling; the average man, washed out by the frustration and grind of the day, spends many evenings slumped in an armchair, gazing into space, while the music that he thinks he enjoys splashes around him like a warm bath.

In this sense, music is quite a good thing. It probably stops many people from going insane and saves a lot of trouble in the world. We shall never know how many minor wars and tribal skirmishes have been prevented by someone knocking hell out of a piano or a primitive drum instead.

You must not, however, be lulled into thinking that music is just simply there to be enjoyed. Music has long been officially recognised and installed as one of the 'arts'. And anything that is an art is no longer a simple pleasure. Arts are a by-product of that general symptom of human decline called civilisation.

Enjoyable pastimes become arts once money is involved. The simple soul who first punched some holes in a bit of bamboo to amuse the kids could never have known what he was letting us all in for.

It seems likely that the first professional musician was the court halhallatu player (reed-pipist) in some ancient Mesopotamian palace – and the chances are that he was heavily criticised in the daily newspapyrus and may even have lost his head as a result.

An art gives employment to a whole lot of people. Someone is bound to make a very rich living out of it and the interesting thing is to see who it is going to be. Once you are paid to do a thing you are open to criticism. Then some people manage to get paid for doing the criticising and they too become open to criticism. Everyone is a critic and cannot imagine why such obvious idiots are allowed to make a living out of messing up the arts which are always, at any given time, going to the dogs anyway.

Instead of music remaining an unassuming accompaniment for foot-and-finger-tapping it becomes a talking (or arguing) point. The whole point of talking about anything is to make the other fellow feel a fool. If you knew the whole of **Grove's** *Dictionary of Music and Musicians* off by heart you could easily make anyone look small. Very few people, however, have the time or money to go to these lengths.

We humbly suggest some short-cuts.

ORDER OF PRECEDENCE

Most important is to get your sense of values right. In music, as in most things, the people involved in the art are far more important than the art itself. If we didn't believe this it would be hard to keep up the struggle.

A great many people are involved in music in one way and another. The main categories in practical order of importance are: **Impresarios**, **Agents**, **etc**; **The B.B.C**; **Recording Companies**; **Conductors**; **Virtuosos (vocal and instrumental)**; **Run-of-the-mill musicians**; **Critics and historians**; **Composers**.

We shall deal with them in this order. Secretly we believe composers to be the most important, but they are difficult to talk about without some preparation. We shall probably devote most time to them. There is no reason why we should not try to be trend-setters.

Impresarios

You might be interested in music all your life and never meet an impresario. They are god-like creatures who tend to live in Bayswater or just off the Finchley Road and they look rather like publishers. Like publishers, too, they are always saying how poor they are although they live in flats and houses full of Picassos and Scarfe cartoons and expensive animals. Our experience is confined to British-based impresarios but no doubt they are much the same the world over.

Impresarios spend most of their lives flying to New York, Moscow, Vienna, Paris and other musical capitals and living in expensive hotels. There are not many of them but, between them, they arrange everything that goes on in the musical world. If they decided tomorrow that Beethoven was not an important composer then Beethoven would be out on his neck. They are unlikely to do this, however, as there is a lot of money yet to be made out of Beethoven.

They refer to musicians by their Christian names so you have to be quite smart to know who they are talking about.

Agents

Agents are the ones who have not made the impresario grade.

The Radio

If it wasn't for the B.B.C. contemporary music would die out, critics would have to buy recordings and scores, professors of music would have to join a union and a whole lot of people would be out of a job.

If you want to be with music of the serious kind then you must listen to the 3rd or Music programme. Not only will you hear the test matches (which most musicians prefer to talk about anyway) but a most astonishing and continuous flood of music which, in normal circumstances, or in the days before traffic jams, you would never have dreamed of listening to.

You will be given an opportunity to hear all Haydn's string quartets, Heckleschmidt's Sonata for fluegel horn and nose flute, and, in the afternoons, all the operas that never get performed on the stage.

In recent times the musical world has been blessed with a new radio experience called Classic FM. This mainly shunts out morsels of classical music of a lightish nature for the education of those who like the bit of music they hear behind advertisements but don't know what it's called. This appears to be working well, even to the extent of persuading people who never went beyond Liberace hitherto to buy recordings of music by obscure Polish composers.

In order to keep the whole thing untainted by any hint of highbrowism, or even intellect, the programme employs Irish disc jockeys who proudly proclaim their ignorance of music, chat about horse racing, and get all the names and titles wrong. Everyone agrees that Classic FM is quite a good thing for everyone else.

Recording Companies

Ever since Tom Edison recorded 'Mary had a little lamb' on a piece of tinfoil way back in 1877 the gramophone record has been winning its way to becoming the most important means of disseminating music.

Nobody is anybody in the musical world until he has made his quota of recordings; and the most sought-after concert artists are those who have recorded most. The ritual of the recording studio has become just as much a part of the routine of a professional musician's life as the concert. Moreover it has shifted the balance of power considerably and put the impresarios' noses not a little out of joint.

True fame only arrives when you have a 'World of ...' or 'Best of ...' album attached to your name. Whereas it was once thought to be the peak of recorded achievement to appear on an exclusive and expensive label, the object now is to get on the cheapest label possible, and in all forms. You are a top conductor if you have managed to persuade your company to let you record all the Beethoven symphonies for the third time; and nowadays Mahler will do just as well.

Not so long ago recording companies were vast conglomerates spending money lavishly and employing many. They got themselves into trouble by promoting tapes and cassette-recorders in the hope of a quick penny, only to find that people were taping their own music from borrowed records and the radio.

Fortunately a new bonanza era arrived with the introduction of the CD which meant that everything had to be re-issued yet again. The recording world is now almost totally run, like everything else, by the Germans and the Japanese, with the British contribution gradually dwindling to a few isolated pockets of resistance in the Welsh foothills and bleak London suburbs.

Recording activities are a favourite topic of conversation amongst the musical. All recordings may be criticised for:

a) not being balanced properly
b) having too much top
c) having too much bottom
d) not having enough music of them and therefore a poor buy
e) having too much music crammed in and therefore of inferior quality
f) a rotten choice of repertoire . . . and so on.

Whereas failings in the concert hall can easily be overlooked or forgotten, failings on record are there for good and for all to hear. If someone praises a new recording you may safely say that the slow movement is too fast, or the finale too slow.

It is not all that much fun being a recording company.

Conductors

more often than not, have their names printed much larger on programmes, posters and covers than the names of the composers – something like this:

WAGGER
CONDUCTS
Wagner
OVERTURES

There is no question that conductors are triumphant, bowing to nobody except impresarios and recording managers. But it wasn't always like that and the history of conducting is a chequered one.

It was realised fairly early on in musical history that it was quite a good idea to have someone beating time so that everyone could play together. The Sistine Choir got such bad crits for their raggedness that someone was delegated to beat time with a roll of paper called a sol-fa. In early Italian opera the leader generally played the harpsichord with one hand and directed with the other. In French operatic circles, however, it soon became the custom for the Master of the Musick to bang on his conducting desk with a stick.

What probably discouraged this practice as much as anything was a rather nasty accident that happened to Lully who was in the habit of using a broom handle to bang on the floor. One day, in an exciting moment during a *Te Deum,* he carelessly banged the broom handle on his big toe. An abscess formed and Lully died soon after.

For some time after this, conductors managed with their bare hands but the dramatic effect was not the same. It was a German composer called Spohr who claimed to be the first to conduct in the modern manner with a baton. From being mere time-beaters, conductors evolved into the martinets that they are today. It was the composers who started it. Bach was a great one for running things his way and Haydn and Mendelssohn were both very fussy about how their music was played. The two conductor/composers who really made a big thing of it were Wagner and Berlioz, the latter even going so far as to write books about it. Nevertheless, it was a bad move on the part of composers to let other people take their place on the rostrum. It provided an ideal outlet for men of domineering tendencies, who were mainly failed composers themselves, to get in on the act.

By the mid-19th century conductors saw themselves as the main reason for having concerts. Dressed in tails and with white gloves and gold-plated batons they gathered huge orchestras together and invented Promenade concerts. A chap called Louis Antoine Jullien started all this.

There are many people who, in fact, after watching a famous conductor are inclined to wonder what he has been there for at all. Couldn't the orchestra do as well without him? If the conductor has done his real work well – that is, the intense browbeating that goes on before the actual performance – it is quite likely that they could do without him on the night.

So the answer to 'What are conductors for?' is: they are there to make the musicians so mad that they will play well just to spite him.

It is all rather like a bull fight: the conductor, the matador; the orchestra, the bull.

As to conductors themselves ... They are simple men. And cowards at heart. It only needs a record producer to stand up to them and they are as meek as lambs. They have simple ambitions – firstly to record all nine Beethoven symphonies – secondly to conduct *Don Giovanni*. They tend to like orchestral musicians on the whole, many having risen from the ranks, and they get on all right with instrumental soloists, but most reluctantly with singers.

If you wish to become a conductor you must be able to silence men with a look, know something about most instruments, and it is a great advantage if your name begins with K though this is not compulsory. The rewards, in this country, are an almost certain knighthood and several honorary degrees – which explains why most British conductors are so well behaved. Beecham, of course, didn't have to worry as his title was hereditary.

Virtuosos

Singers

It has been said that the only trouble with singers is that they just cannot keep their mouths shut. Conversely, many critics have been known to complain that they do.

The real trouble with singers, however, is split personality. If they just confine themselves to singing they are all right. But nearly all singers, because of that monstrous convention known as opera, are also called upon to be actors. And we all know what actors are like.

Singers have to live with this sense of failure to become actors, and make up for it by behaving like tennis players. There is an eternal war between singers and conductors – a battle for supremacy; and only the impresario or the recording manager can control the situation by waving his cheque-book.

A quick dip into any critique will give you a handful of phrases to use in connection with singers. Here are some good ones: 'colourless above the stave', 'well-schooled but dull', 'tone hardens under pressure', 'light of voice', 'lacking a sense of style', 'studied eloquence', 'ugly vibrato'. Perfection in singing is never acknowledged. There are so many nasty things to say that the veriest amateur amongst us can find something.

While conductors and pianists of today are often con-sidered the equal of, or even better than, the precarious technicians of the past, and orchestral musicians are definitely considered to have at last got the hang of their instruments, singers are, like cricketers and policemen, definitely considered to have deteriorated. The art of **bel canto** (simply and unmysteriously 'beautiful singing') is dead. All that we have to uphold this decision is the evidence of nostalgic memoir-writers and those croaking early 78s which merely suggest that everyone then sang out of tune; but the myth exists and singers must learn to live with it. The fact is that we can now hear them so well that their faults are only too evident.

Apart from opera, singers have so many dull songs written for them (these are generally called **Lieder**) that they are at a great disadvantage compared with the concerto-type musician and, for some reason, the sort of music that makes singers sound happiest, like Mahler's *Des Knaben Wunderhorn* and Brahms's *Liebeslieder* waltzes, is comparatively rarely heard. This looks like a conspiracy on the part of conductors.

The greatest achievement in singing is to become a well-loved contralto. The un-loved ones generally end up singing Gilbert & Sullivan.

Pianists

exist to play piano **concertos.** They play other things as well, of course, like chamber music and sonatas, impromptus, bagatelles and snooker, but the piano concertos are the most important things in modern music-making and it is impossible to stage them properly without presentable pianists. Pianists, therefore, look far more like composers ought to look, according to romantic convention, and are just as impressive as conductors. All successful pianists know all the twenty top concertos off by heart. Impresarios simply ring them up and say 'B3 – Simon – 15 June AH' and all the famous pianist need say in reply is 'How much?' He may haggle a bit at this point but not over the music.

Don't think that it is easy to become a great piano concertist. Apart from several hours practice a day, regularly soaking the hands in hot olive oil and insuring them for thousands of pounds, he has to practise adjustment of piano stools, flinging tails over the back of the piano stool neatly and accurately, hand-wringing, brow-mopping, looking interesting and unconcerned during the moments when he is not actually playing, shaking hands with conductors and leaders, taking encores and bowing.

Most pianists are heartily sick of playing and recording the top twenty concertos. In common with conductors, they like to do their Beethoven set and most would happily embark on all 27 of Mozart's, but generally get discouraged with regard to this pleasant bit of extravagance. The other thing that all pianists like to record is a set of the Chopin waltzes.

Pianists are easy prey to criticism. One should immediately cast doubts on their touch – 'shadowy, featherweight, not firm enough', are some of the criticisms to make in one direction – 'hamfisted, cluttered, inflexible, leaden, exhibitionist' in the other.

Pianists nearly always ignore the composer's **dynamic** markings – that is to say, they play soft where they should play loud and vice versa. Pedal markings, too, they treat as quite a joke – what right, they say, have composers to tell us pianists when to use the pedals? They are very like motorists in this respect.

But the main disease that afflicts pianists is **rubato.** Rubato is a pulling about of the tempo, a lingering over emotional bits, a rushing of already hectic passages. Victorian pianists loved rubato to the point of mania. They applied it especially to Chopin. The critics waded in, for once, to such good effect that lately pianists have given up rubato almost entirely – except for a few of the older ones. Now they dash through Chopin with unswerving precision and unfluctating speeds so that it all sounds like a piano roll. Like punctuation of any kind – rubato should be used, but always in moderation. A very good talking point, indeed.

Organists

are a strange race. Quite apart from their unusual physical make-up which allows them to use their two hands and two feet independently, playing on several keyboards at once and manipulating countless stops, they are most definitely in the superman class. Not even a conductor wields such power over such a massive instrument – often spreading itself all over one side of a cathedral. Yet with all that power in their hands they prefer to play long rambling toccatas and fugues of luculent dullness from the mustiest-looking of all music books. Their journals and books are full of the most wearying technicalities, and naturally have more footnotes than most.

Don't mess with organists or even attempt to discuss them. They are a race apart and their music is not of this world.

Violinists

are continually frustrated by the size and capacity of their instruments. While pianists entirely depend on the manipulation of ten fingers and anything up to 88 black and white notes, violinists have to make do with five fingers and four strings. Getting awfully bored with playing on one string at a time, they have a constant urge to play on two or more. This always sounds horrible even when done by a very good violinist. The reason would seem to be **enharmonics.** The piano uses a tempered scale in which D♯ and E♭ are the same note. The physical nature of sounds and acute conservatism says that they are not. The slight difference is something that violinists imagine they can hear. However, when they come to play two notes together this involves some pretty horrible near harmonies. They love it. They rewrite brief and simple cadenzas, carefully supplied by the best composers, making them long and full of double and treble stopping (as they like to refer to their playing of two or more strings). At the moment it is a lawful practice. So there is nothing much we can do about it.

Violinists have only about ten top concertos and a much smaller repertoire in general than pianists. They are always arranging other sorts of music for violin and have never yet been known to make it sound better than it was in its original form. But still they persist.

The most cutting thing you can do about violinists is to call them fiddlers. The truth always hurts.

MUSICIANS

are the stalwarts who make up the chief orchestras of the world and always play magnificently under any conditions. Between times they take off their wigs and provide the lush backings that are considered essential for pop groups and commercials.

There are only sixty top run-of-the-mill musicians in London and each one works a 22-hour day and gets rich on overtime.

Orchestral musicians on the whole are very jaded people, and the minute the music-making stops for a moment, they pick up a thriller or a newspaper or start practising their golf swings. They are also members of a union and, as anyone knows in this country, if you are a member of a union your whole philosophy of life is to work less for more money. Any right-wing paper will tell you that.

Contrary to general belief there is no difference between amateur and professional musicians: they all suffer from the same bad habits and foibles. It is just that the amateurs need more practice.

Did you know, by the way, that if a modern French Horn was straightened out it would be too long to take on a bus? It is not worth trying to prove this as they are very expensive instruments. Even the ordinary Bassoon, if it was not bent, would be about nine feet long. If the average orchestral musician was straightened out what on earth would he do for a living?

CRITICS

are all failed composers or musicians and therefore know better than anything else what failure is and tend to harp on it. When they suddenly find themselves agreeing, they are greatly surprised and overdo it.

The Achilles heel of critics is their commitment to print. Things said in anger (really directed against PAYE in a lot of cases) are immutably there to be quoted against them for the rest of their lives. Consider the case of Mr. Krehbiel, an American critic who in 1907 wrote of Debussy's *La Mer*:

> 'Last night's concert began with a lot of impressionistic daubs of colour smeared higgledy-piggledy on a tonal palette, with never a thought of form or purpose except to create new combinations of sounds . . . One thing only was certain, and that was that the composer's ocean was a frog-pond, and that some of its denizens had got into the throat of every one of the brass instruments.'

We may believe that Mr. Krehbiel was unabashed when he wrote of Debussy's *La Mer* in 1922:

> 'A poetic work in which Debussy has so wonderfully caught the rhythms and colours of the sea.'

But don't you believe it. He was as abashed as a man could be and only hoped that nobody would remember.

Some critics by a mere torrent of words have managed to live down such slips as made by George Bernard Shaw when he spoke of Schubert's C major Symphony as an 'exasperatingly brainless composition' or Ernest Newman when he likened Mozart's music to 'the nursery prattlings of a bright child'. They both shone at a time when it was good to be a critic because **bel canto** had only just died and orchestral players did not know their job. They often played out of tune and it was the critic's pleasurable privilege to say so. Nowadays they don't.

INSTRUMENTAL ODDS & ENDS

One of the most effective things to say with regard to concertos by composers like Bach and up to about Haydn, is 'but of course it should not be played on the piano'; quickly followed by the remark that 'it is clearly written for the harpsichord'. This always works because very few people, even experts, are entirely clear in their minds as to when the piano really took over.

There were references to the *piano e forte* way back in the 16th century, the basic idea being a keyboard instrument that could play both soft and loud. Bartolomeo Cristofori had quite a good instrument for sale soon after 1700, but its name stood in the way. People just didn't like going into a shop and saying 'could I have one of those *gravecembalo col piano e fortes*, please – and will you take a cheque?' Cristofori kept trying, however, and had got the idea off the ground by about 1725.

Although most of the early pianos sounded like those to be found in Second World War canteens (and many survive in present-day village halls), composers like C.P.E. Bach, Mozart and Clementi all took to it early in their careers. With regard to them you can say 'but of course they shouldn't be played on a modern piano', i.e. a piano that sounds pleasant. It is best not to pursue the matter further than that.

The saxophone is so-called because it was invented by a Mr. Sax (first name Antoine Joseph but known to his friends as Adolphe). It was patented by him in 1846. This is not a joke, but serious information. An occasional hard fact is a good conversational gambit. Having established this, you can go on to say that the xylophone was invented by a Mr. Xyl, and the gramophone by a Mr. Gram – but don't get carried away.

CONVERSATION PIECE

A conversation between two people unhappily thrown together at a party by a hostess who knows that both have a modest collection of records.

A. Were you at Winkelski's recital on Tuesday?
B. Indeed I was. What did you think of the B minor?
A. I wasn't too impressed. I think he's much more at home with the E flat.
B. Oh, really. Surely Richter is the man for that?
A. Yes and no. He always plays the allegro too fast for my liking and could give it a shade more rubato.
B. Winkelski has a wonderful ear for detail.
A. He has a firm touch but lacks variety.
B. And tends to ignore the composer's dynamic markings.
A. He is more at home in music of a deeper chromatic hue.
B. Like the Brahms 2.
A. Exactly.

You can sense that neither has the faintest idea what the other really means (or what he means himself, for that matter). The conversation has the quality of detergent froth on a river. They now proceed to go through a long list of composers and performers, casting aspersions on the results of years of study and practice, only occasionally granting a word of mild approbation.

You can tell they are not professional critics. If they were, the conversation would go more like this:

A. Were you at the Festival Hall on Tuesday?
B. I'm afraid so. Absolute chaos in the B minor.
A. Ought to stick to Liszt.
B. They wanted him to do the E flat but he wouldn't.
A. Clot.
B. Couldn't get a bloody coffee in the interval.
A. What a waste of time. See you at Lord's tomorrow?

COMPOSERS

It is generally agreed, very reluctantly, that composers are also essential to music. There are four composers who are beyond criticism – Bach, Beethoven, Mozart and your own particular favourite. To attempt to criticise one of these would be as fruitless as saying that Shakespeare was a poor dramatist or that you cannot see why people make such a fuss about The Beatles. There is no need to say that you admire Beethoven or Mozart because this is assumed. Bach is a slightly different matter – *see below*. As for your own choice, you will have to defend him (strange how negligible the female contribution to music has been) with your life, for once people know that you have a passion for anything they will do their best to destroy it. You will notice, incidentally, that no young or progressive critics will mention Beethoven or Mozart if they can possibly help it.

Beethoven

is regarded as a public company in which a number of people have shares and it is important to know how many shares each of them holds. Thus one talks of Klemperer's Beethoven, Karajan's Beethoven, Solti's Beethoven, Bernstein's Beethoven and, after a bit of research, Furtwängler's Beethoven – those are the main shareholders, with Klemperer holding a working majority. All conductors have an inner compulsion to record a complete cycle of Beethoven's symphonies. Some achieve it but some get stuck half way.

The only fruitful line of discussion on Beethoven is

with regard to the comparative merits of the symphonies. The concertos are rarely mentioned, especially the *Emperor* and the Violin Concerto because they are both perfect and popular and lead the conversation nowhere.

The symphony above criticism is the 3rd, the *Eroica*. It is ineffably great but should be avoided at Promenade concerts when, for some reason, it tends to become ineffably long and consequently a bore. However, the *Eroica* need not personally be blamed; merely be content to say what a shambles the conductor in question has made of this great masterpiece.

The 5th and 6th symphonies have both become far too popular and most people can actually hum bits from them after only a very brief hesitation. The 9th, the *Choral* is rather dangerous ground and it is best to steer the conversation away from it. No-one, apart from Vaughan Williams, has yet made up his mind about the 9th and it is liable to put the talk on a serious level. It brings in the well-established fallacy that Beethoven could not write for the voice and will lead on to murky discussion about *Fidelio* and the choral works.

You can be condescendingly affectionate towards No. 1, and No. 2 – a Beethoven hot tip, usually getting overlooked and the least recorded, but a delightful work. The fashionable symphonies have been 4, 7 and 8, although 8 is almost too good to be true. Odd-numbered symphonies of Beethoven have always been a little over-admired and it says much for 7's strength of character that it has always managed to be slightly less-loved than 3, 5 or 9. Go for it in a big way.

The really serious Beethoven enthusiast will deeply admire the piano sonatas or the quartets. The sonatas were taken over long ago by Artur Schnabel and anyone who deviates from what he did with them is slightly suspect. The efforts of such poachers on these preserves as Ashkenazy, Brendel, Barenboim, Arrau or John Lill must be treated, therefore, as plus or minus so many degrees Schnabel.

The quartets on the other hand are anyone's meat and you have every right to be very severe with anyone who tries to play them at all. It may correctly be assumed that no-one can ever do the job properly. Actual discussion of the quartets themselves should be left to the experts.

Useful items to trot out casually in terms of affectionate familiarity: Romances for violin and orchestra, No. 1 in G, Op. 40; No. 2 in F, Op. 50; Septet in E♭, Op. 20 – a real charmer; Quintet for piano and wind in E♭, Op. 16; and a passing acquaintance with the notebooks makes a good impression.

Mozart

had the unique distinction, as everyone knows, of writing Koechels instead of Opuses, a thing no other composer has done before or since. Mozart's great popularity dates from the time that this absorbing fact was discovered, by some strange coincidence, by a man called Koechel (pronounced 'kir-kel'). These numbers add a wonderful air of mystery to his works, though as might be expected, they can be quite a hazard if not handled properly. Although no-one would be expected to know Beethoven's Opus numbers and would be considered slightly mad if they knew all Bach's BWV numbers, it is a very good thing to be on familiar terms with a few Koechels.

People have made quick reputations by being able to compare, in a casual way, K.375b with K.375c. It is fairly safe to do this sort of thing as the odds are pretty high against anybody being in a position to contradict you.

There are some numbers that you must know – for instance K.525. It is a sad affliction to have to go around referring to the *Eine kleine Nachtmusik* although you can get away with calling it Serenade No. 13.

You ought also to know K.385 – the *Haffner* symphony, K.425 the *Linz,* K.504 the *Prague* and K.551 the *Jupiter* – never, never refer to these symphonies by their numbers except abroad – also, K.543 which is Symphony No. 39 and K.550 which is No. 40 – never refer to these by their names as they haven't got any.

You might make a start by knowing what K.100, K.200, K.300, K.400 and K.500 are, but this is rather an obvious trick. A good one is K.365 which is the E♭ Concerto for two pianos, 365 being, you may remember, the number of days in an average year.

Every now and then somebody comes along and messes about with the Mozart numerology. It is all good clean fun, and nobody takes any notice of it.

Nobody ever refers to Piano concerto No. 23 unless he wants to be thought really dated. If you cannot remember that it is K.488 then refer to it as *the* A major concerto. The fact that there are others in A major leaves your opponent in quite an uneasy state and even more confused if you say 'the' instead of *the*. (*NB:* be careful not to be trapped into a discussion of Symphony No. 34 which Mozart got somebody else to write as he was feeling a bit off-colour that day.)

A few other hot tips for numbers are K.297b – the E♭ Sinfonia Concertante, K.622, the Clarinet concerto and K.264 which is 9 piano variations on 'Lison dormait'.

You will soon acquire some obscure favourites of your own.

You may think that we have slightly exaggerated the importance of this number business. There is, however, little else that you can say about Mozart, for everything he wrote is perfect with never a wrong note in it. The proper reaction to Mozart is to go glassy-eyed and full of inexpressible admiration.

If you find Mozart's music boring you had better keep this horrible fact to yourself. You might as well say that you don't like animals or you can't see the point of cricket.

One of the most pleasing things about Mozart is that hardly anyone can perform his music very well. Conductors who shatter us with their Beethoven, browbeat us with their Wagner and belay us with their Bartók, get so nervous when they perform Mozart that you can be absolutely certain that 95 per cent of Mozart performances are unsatisfactory – so do not hesitate to say so. As the ideal seems to be an orchestra of angels with St. Peter conducting and Mozart himself playing the piano, it is quite clear why mere mortals so often fail.

Useful offbeat Mozart works include: the ballet music *Les Petits Riens*, K.299b; Sinfonia concertante in E♭, K.364; the Bassoon concerto, K.191; the Wind quintet, K.452; Serenade No. 10 for 13 wind instruments, K.361; Serenade No. 4 in D, K.203 and the song 'Moto di gioia', K.579 – plus any number of German dances and minuets that you can remember. As a special treat try Beecham's recording of K.605, No. 3.

Incidentally, Mozart was a jolly good chap. He was quite as ugly as you or me, had a passion for beer and billiards and always had an overdraft. How much nearer to perfection can a composer get?

Bach

we approach with some trepidation. Bach is not really a mere musical commodity at all, but a religion. He is adored by all intellectual virgins (male or female). Like cold showers and hot baths, Bach's music is an almost satisfactory substitute for sex. Its purity grips minds slightly too rarified to be properly religious. It must be listened to, sung, played and discussed with an expression of ineluctable piety. Compared with the music of Bach, Beethoven's and Mozart's efforts are the soiled product of the dirty human hand.

It is possible to like Bach and nothing else – it is even likely. Yet in spite of the clinical and demanding nature of his music it is tremendously popular. If you meet a real Bach addict it would be better to faint or pretend that you have to get home because of the baby-sitter. Any suggestion that you can take Bach as good clean fun can earn you a very nasty reputation. You must take Bach seriously or not at all.

Fortunately there is only one remark that is necessary in normal conversation and that is 'Ah . . . Bach!' We realise that this is very unhelpful but if you stick to that one remark, with varying inflections, it would seem the safest course to take and covers all emergencies.

One can feel sorry for Bach, privately, for one thing: he has been afflicted with **BWV** numbers, great ugly things with not a breath of poetry about them. It is unfair that any composer should be lumbered with such a typographical curse.

There is not much that you can say in a critical spirit about his life. As a youth he walked more than 400 miles to hear Buxtehude play the organ. Not even standing through a Promenade concert can equal that for musical devotion. After this initial penance he settled down to a life of hard work, most of it spent at the keyboard and writing an unremitting flood of music, all of it clever and clean. He also managed to have eleven children. What else can one say about such a man except 'Ah . . . Bach!'

Those not addicted to everything that Bach wrote might try: Concerto in D minor for oboe, violin and strings, BWV.1060; *Italian* concerto in F, BWV.971 or *'Wachet auf'* arr. piano or orchestra.

OTHER COMPOSERS

All other composers are a little less than gods. Unlike Beethoven, Mozart and Bach, who seem superhuman by normal standards, the following were all ordinary men and may be treated with affable contempt and in alphabetical order.

Bartók

is great stuff for people with the kind of mentality that takes naturally to chess and Ximenes crosswords. There is nothing actually pleasant about his music but standing up to it gives one the same exhilarating satisfaction as bathing in a cold and rough sea or watching a test match. Indeed, it has been statistically proved that something like 88 per cent of the people who actually enjoy watching cricket are also very fond of Bartók.

There is no need to look for obscure Bartók for it is all that way inclined. Know the Concerto for Orchestra; the Music for strings, percussion and celesta; and Piano concerto No. 3 and your success is assured.

Berlioz

is a man to distrust because he was so professional about it all. He knew exactly what he was doing and wrote large books about it which has made him very unpopular amongst critics and historians who do not like composers flaunting their literacy.

He wrote the kind of music that is very suitable as background and signature tunes for TV programmes, which confirms many people's suspicions that he was always going to the dogs anyway. He was almost certainly in league with the Devil and, in fact, received 20,000 francs from him, sent via Paganini, one of the Devil's right-hand men. The *Symphonie Fantastique* is used quite regularly nowadays at some of the best sabbaths and bears out the fact that the Devil has all the best tunes. You may secretly admire and even enjoy Berlioz's works and build a naughty little reputation as a musical sensualist.

We are sorry to have to point out that works like the overtures *Les Francs Juges* and *Roman Carnival* are harmlessly enjoyable. To be really smart suggest a casual acquaintance with *The Trojans* and follow their line of attack. If this fails you can always claim to have met Colin Davis at a party.

Brahms

is a fellow you cannot help liking even if some of his music seems unutterably cluttered. He was a comfortably fat man with a big bushy beard rather like Edward Lear or W. G. Grace and he often conducted with one hand in his pocket – jingling the money that he had got in advance. He wished he had written Johann Strauss's waltzes – then he would really have had something to jingle. He would also have liked to have written symphonies like Beethoven's, but whenever he set out to do so he inevitably got confused and the works got very long and involved and he lost count of the number of instruments he was writing for.

On the whole he had an uneventful life which he tried to brighten by being quietly rude to most people and by collecting tin soldiers. He did things that a lot of people would have liked to have done – like falling asleep while Liszt was playing the piano – and he used to make jokes at parties about Wagner. He refused to come to England on the grounds that Englishmen did not smoke good cigars. Taking your cue from Brahms himself, you may be very rude about his music and no-one will mind in the least.

Most women adore Brahms's symphonies and these hardly need recommending. The only person who could knock them into cohesive shape was Toscanini.

Least known and doubly satisfying is his Concerto in A minor for Violin and Cello, Op. 102. The *Hungarian Dances* should only be admired in their original form as piano duets, likewise the delightful Waltzes, Op. 39. For a curious pleasure and a perverse taste in Brahms cultivate the *Liebeslieder Walzer*, Op. 52 and dabble in the Lieder.

Britten

wrote the kind of music that always sounds as if it is going to break into a tune – but doesn't. He wrote two kinds of works; vocal, which all sound as if they were written for Peter Pears to sing (and were), and non-vocal, which all sound as if they were written for Peter

Pears to sing (and may have been but he was busy at the time). In fact there is some ground for believing that Benjamin Britten wrote *Peter Pears*, as an early opera with one act.

Britten wrote uncompromisingly modern (but mainly **diatonic**) music and turned it out with a regularity and artistic acumen only equalled by Rossini in his productive days. There ought to be some way of dismissing his work lightly. But its peculiar personal poetry, (a mixture of Grimm's fairy tales and Peter Pears) is so utterly compelling that everyone has been forced to admit that he was probably a real genius.

His musical emotional world has been summed up as 'a deep nostalgia for the innocence of childhood' (a liking for boys' choirs), 'a mercurial sense of humour' (obsession with death and war) and 'a passionate sympathy with the victims of prejudice or misunderstanding' (Peter Pears).

Bruch

is known to the average music-lover as the man who wrote Violin Concerto No. 1 in G Minor, Op. 26 and some cello variations on *Kol Nidrei,* Op. 47. A nodding acquaintance with his other ninety compositions would be impressive but boring. Riemann, in his Dictionary of 1922, stated that the best of Bruch was to be found in his choral works and there is no known reason why this should not be repeated ad nauseam. Peers' dismissal of him as the 'babbling Bruch' does, however, seem a little harsh.

Bruckner

It is generally said that Bruckner was a very simple man – practically a nature boy, you would gather from some writers. If, after listening to one of his symphonies, you still feel that he was simple, then you are not the kind of person who should be reading this book. In fact, Bruckner was as deep as the ocean. He was also an organist and organists (*q.v.*) are far from simple men.

Another misrepresentation of Bruckner is to bracket him with Mahler. The only thing they had in common was a liking for long symphonies. And whereas Mahler really wanted people to like and enjoy his symphonies, Bruckner could not have cared less. In the midst of all the musical money-making that was going on in Vienna at the end of the 19th century Bruckner quietly enjoyed himself writing long, unapproachable symphonies and went out of his way to look unartistic with short hair and a moustache. Only Elgar has ever looked less musical.

When Bruckner had written his symphonies he let anybody play about with them, which a lot of longhaired musicologists were only too keen to do – having never actually got down to writing more than the first eight bars of a long symphony themselves. These chaps, having money and influence, got the symphonies played so that they could hear their own bits. One should therefore always demand unsullied Bruckner – never accept a Bruckner symphony unless it bears the wording 'an Anton Bruckner original' and is full of Bruckner's unmistakable simplicities.

The 4th is the nice symphony; the rest you can take your choice with. Bruckner just didn't write pleasant little recommendable pieces.

Chopin

is coming back into fashion after being made to appear a trifling sentimentalist by hosts of Victorian pianists. He is also gradually living down the fact that he led an inordinately romantic life with a lady novelist, died young in the approved manner and wrote 'I'm always chasing rainbows' and 'How deep is the night'.

There was almost a feeling abroad in recent years that Chopin ought not to be encouraged and that the fellow was debasing the hard currency of music. But pianists since Rubinstein, who played him with steely fingers on hard-toned pianos with great speed and brilliance, have persuaded us that Chopin is every bit as good as Liszt – if not better. Chopin himself had no doubts on the matter and described Liszt as 'a clever craftsman without a vestige of talent'. It looks as if we must forgive him for being so unforgettably melodic and thoroughly entertaining.

Chopin admirers plump for the least unbending of his works like the Etudes and the Preludes, but if you enjoy the Waltzes and the Polonaises just jolly well say so and, surprisingly, you may get away with it.

Profess an admiration for the Cello sonata in G minor, Op. 65 and a great disdain for the blasphemous *Les Sylphides* even if you secretly enjoy it. Another enjoyable work is the Introduction and Polonaise in C for cello and piano, Op. 3.

Still quite a good ploy is to admire Chopin as a composer for cello.

Debussy

See under Critics.

Delius

suffered all his life from being the son of a German born Bradford wool merchant. His family wanted him in the wool business but the ridiculousness of this for one of his artistic bent was obvious and he went to Florida to grow oranges instead. This venture failing, he passed quickly through England, avoiding Bradford, and went to live on the Continent, finally settling in France.

It is perhaps truer of Delius's music than that of any other composer that you either like it or you don't. All rights in Delius's music were bought up by Beecham and nobody else has been allowed to play it properly since. In fact his music is like a French impressionist's painting of Romney Marsh and nobody can quite account for Beecham's addiction to it.

Ending his life paralysed and blind as the result of contracting the composers' favourite disease*, he employed a young musician called Eric Fenby (subsequently referred to as an amanuensis – which doesn't sound very nice) to write down his final compositions.

After his death Delius was partly forgiven for not wanting to live in England and his remains were reburied in a Surrey churchyard.

---

* It has been estimated by one tireless researcher that more composers contract syphilis than any other occupation. This could lead to an interesting discussion – even wild speculation.

Dvořák

was a hard-working son of a pork butcher and looked
like one himself. With a head full of dance rhythms and
country melodies he went amiably through life writing
countless works and giving them all the wrong opus
numbers. He spent two years in America and actually
enjoyed the experience – turning it to good account by
writing his best-seller there – the *New World* symphony. Dvořák's music is so full of Bohemian atmos-
phere that practically all orchestras can make a pretty
good job of it – but only the Czech Philharmonic can
really tear the heart out of it.

The only faults that one can find with Dvořák are his
inordinate admiration for Brahms and Wagner, which
sometimes made him try to write their works instead of
his own, and those tiresome accents which printers
nearly always get wrong.

Some special Dvořákian delights are the String
serenade, Op. 22; the *Scherzo capriccioso,* Op. 66; the
Piano quintet, Op. 81 and the *Dumky* trio, Op. 90.

Elgar

was an incredibly English Englishman who could easily
have been a major-general if he had wanted to with
hardly any effort on his part.

After a youth happily misspent riding a bicycle up
and down the Malvern Hills he suddenly achieved fame
by writing his *Enigma* variations. Each variation represented one of his friends and after clever folk had
discovered who all these were they then wanted to know
what the variations were variations on. In fact, Elgar
himself had forgotten but had to pretend that he wanted
to keep it a secret.

He then wrote the *Pomp and Circumstance* marches and got very depressed whenever he heard *Land of Hope and Glory* being played at Waterloo Station.

He managed to become the most typical of all English composers by demonstrating a marked preference for going to the races, rather than writing music which always tended to make him rather irritable. Much misunderstood and misplayed in his lifetime he has become a pillar of English musical respectability and the Three Choirs Festival.

There is not much point in trying to pose as an expert on Elgar as nearly everybody has done it already.

Grieg

like Dvořák, was an amiable little man who wished no-one any harm. Being very small he mostly wrote very small works – the outstanding exception being his Piano Concerto which is No. 1 in the classical hit parade. More records of this work are sold than of any other. It is imperative therefore to keep off the concerto and find hidden delights in his other pieces – of which there are plenty.

The most remarkable thing he did was to write incidental music to Ibsen's weird play *Peer Gynt* – music of such dramatic unsuitability that it and the play decided to part company many years ago. The pleasantness of the music must have induced many people to go and see *Peer Gynt* and to get a bit of a shock.

Most likeable Grieg after these pieces are the *Holberg* suite, Op. 40; and the *Norwegian dances,* Op. 35, preferably in their original piano duet form.

Handel

kindly left behind him some *Water Music* (eternally useful for all aquatic occasions), some *Firework Music* (for pyrotechnic displays of any kind) and *Messiah* (for the regular occasions when choral societies want to get a good audience and raise some money).

In spite of this we are ungratefully inclined to say that he dominated English music for so long that he almost made the native breed of composer extinct. It was only Elgar and *Land of Hope and Glory* that eventually saved the situation.

Haydn

was the father of the symphony. Contrary to the usual way of life, no-one knew who the mother was. Haydn decided that symphonies should have beginnings and middles and ends, first movements in sonata forms and minuets and trios. Beethoven, in his usual churlish way, disregarded and spoilt this nice conventional plan.

The general feeling is that Haydn could have been as good as Mozart if he had not been so incurably happy for most of his life. This spirit of contentment got into all his music and diluted it. His last few symphonies he wrote in London for ready cash and the cloud of the contract hanging over him added that little spice of misery that had been lacking before. Perhaps only a really heartless man could have written anything so incredibly happy as the finale of Symphony No. 88.

There are lots of virtually unplayed symphonies that you can claim as a special favourite, but the best remark about Haydn is that all his best music is in the masses – there is no need to say of what.

Liszt

was described by Chopin as 'an excellent binder who puts other people's works between the covers'. About two-thirds of the prodigious amount of music he wrote was other people's. He was a confirmed arranger and could have done well financially in any age. He took other men's music (the simpler the better) and then filled up all the spaces with masses of black notes, thick chords, runs that hardly anyone but he could play, impossible octaves, ridiculous leaps. He recoiled in horror when he saw a plain tune in all its nakedness and hastened to swathe it in decent arpeggios. He saw all music as a great eternal cadenza.

At heart Liszt was a pianist rather than a composer and, like all pianists, thought the best bit of a concerto was when the whole orchestra and the conductor sat in mute silence while the soloist used the piano like an exhibition skater on television.

In between bouts of enjoying being the greatest pianist in the world and eating caviare Liszt would become disgusted with the whole racket and do penitential things like giving all his money away, turning to religion and encouraging Wagner. Then he would have the urge to get back to the gay life again and rush off on another successful concert tour quite forgetting that he was still dressed like a bishop.

In his later years he sobered down and wrote some complicated music of his own and became known as the Abbé Liszt. The composers never forgave him and it took years for them to get their works played in their original forms again. Critics have finally forgiven him and diagnosed his case as acute schizophrenia. Pieces like *La campanella* (pinched from Paganini) and the *Grand marche chromatique* are now considered great fun.

Mahler

had an incurable ambition to write the longest, noisiest and most expensive symphonies in the world (expensive because they need so many people to perform them). This he achieved and, not surprisingly, it was a long time before people could be persuaded to listen to them or impresarios felt like trying to make them do so.

It was suddenly realised that Mahler had not written big long boring symphonies of the Brahms type which you have to listen to carefully from beginning to end in order not to miss the themes, but had, in fact, simply strung together hundreds of attractive little tunes, and it was possible to go into a coma for a lot of the symphony and still get involved when you came to again. It is possible to switch on the car radio in the depths of Surrey to what appears to be a Mahler symphony well in its stride and to arrive in London and find a parking place with it still going on in a forgetfully energetic way that suggests it might still be in progress at 5.30. It is quite obvious that all conductors get lost during a work like the 7th which one writer, we forget which, once dubbed the 'Mad'. No doubt somebody will prove one day that Mahler *was* crazy. If not, why did he go to such trouble to write so much when he achieved better results in his short symphonies like the 1st and 4th?

It is said that he had a thing about writing a 9th but it was probable that he was getting tired as he was holding down a steady job as conductor. His chances of having an 'Unfinished' symphony were thwarted by Deryck Cooke, who kindly finished off his 10th for him.

Mahler has almost become too fashionable but there is still plenty to talk about. Latch on to a fleeting theme in the middle of the 8th and say it reminds you of 'Pop goes the weasel' and few will care to argue.

Mendelssohn

is definitely considered to have unmatured. He wrote all his best works when he was about 17 – such as the Octet and the overture to *A Midsummer Night's Dream*. At the advanced age of 24 he pulled himself together sufficiently to write his *Italian* symphony; but thereafter only managed to write drawing-room pieces for the piano and large choral works that served as a model for all the bad Victorian English music that followed. He was approved of by Queen Victoria which was sufficient cause for condemnation by all the highbrow critics.

A good line with Mendelssohn is a spirited defence of his Piano concertos which not many people know, especially the double concertos. Definitely keep off the *Hebrides* overture which has a strong smell of the Albert Hall about it.

Rachmaninov

was a gaunt, sad man of Lisztian mould torn between the fruitful occupation of being a lion-pianistique and the humbler duties of a composer. He compromised neatly by writing concertos (including No. 2 in the world's top ten) and playing them much better than anyone else ever could. Critics were always saying he was finished; but, just as they had finally written him off, he wrote *Rhapsody on a theme of Paganini* which is the world's best loved pseudoconcerto. (One cannot help being sorry for Paganini – as a composer he has never been rated very highly yet seemed to supply a lending library of themes for everyone else).

The Russian authorities said that Rachmaninov's music represented 'the decadent attitude of the lower middle classes'. Had they attended the Proms, they would have been gratified to find out how right they were.

Schoenberg

started out in quite a normal way by orchestrating operettas which he did quite well. Having decided to be a serious composer he began by trying to write music like Wagner and Brahms but then discovered that Wagner and Brahms had done it already. After a few lengthy and abortive attempts in this direction he concluded that he would have to find a different method. Idly toying with a crossword puzzle one day he came up with the idea of writing music to a formula that would make inspiration unnecessary. He took the twelve notes of the **chromatic** scale in a random order using each of them once. Provided that they stuck to that order he made up new rules, like being able to play them backwards or sideways or standing on your head. For the sake of variety you could even cheat.

At first this all sounded very novel and the idea was taken up by all the other composers who couldn't write better music than Wagner or Brahms – or even Schoenberg. Since then twelve-note music has become the salvation of the second-rate and those who lack imagination. It was sad for Schoenberg that his scheme for getting away from the limitations of the old music produced something that was even more limiting and whose overwhelming characteristic was a sameness, whoever wrote it. Schoenberg can at least be credited with being the man who did more than anyone to create a public appetite for old and hackneyed music, and an endless demand for the Grieg and Tchaikovsky piano concertos. It is rather unfair that his name should be used by music-loving parents to frighten naughty children.

A declared liking for Schoenberg must gain ready admiration but will make you few friends.

Schubert

is the one composer that everyone enjoys without
needing to bracket him with Beethoven or Bach. By
academic standards he was probably a bit naïve and
insisted on cramming melodies into nearly everything
that he wrote. He liked clean, bouncy rhythms and
accompaniments that stuck to definite patterns – a sort
of early 19th century 'boogie' addict. Even Schubert
couldn't maintain his inspiration all the time and he
wrote hundreds of songs that only occasionally get
trotted out at a recital or in a Fischer-Dieskau collection
– but at least a hundred of them have that memorable
perfection that the world craves. He was very keen, too,
on abrupt modulations into other keys, but these sound
harmless nowadays in an age where keys are pretty
well done for.

Schubert's symphonies up to No. 6 are in the
Mozartian style. At this point he began to suffer from a
dislike of symphonies and he never got around to doing
anything more than some preliminary sketches for No.
7 and then started on No. 8 in a fine burst of enthusiasm
but never finished it. To make up for this slacking he
wrote an extra long and rather rambling 9th.

Schubert's symphonies, being so endearingly simple
on the whole, suffer in performance in the way that
Mozart's do and very rarely does anyone come up with a
really worthwhile interpretation. Beecham could, of
course, but practically no-one else.

One does not refer to Schubert's 'songs', by the way,
but to his **Lieder.** This is a pity because they are really
songs. Lots of other people like Schumann, Brahms,
Strauss and Wolf wrote Lieder but Schubert definitely
wrote songs.

Johann Strauss

wrote hundreds of waltzes, polkas, mazurkas and operettas most of which are very unlikely to be heard again. He used the permutatory method of composition – the constant rearrangement of groups of notes until something good materialised. Approximately one in every thirty of his compositions turned out to be a masterpiece. A very arduous way of achieving results, but quite feasible for a dance-band leader like Strauss who presumably had lots of time on the coach between dates. Duke Ellington had a similar liking for composing while in transit.

His good waltzes are very good and Strauss may now be spoken of in the most select musical company without any condescension. Likewise *Die Fledermaus* and *The Gypsy Baron* – two of the most perfect operettas ever written.

Richard Strauss

probably much regretted that he was not Johann Strauss (he was not even a relation) and wrote *Der Rosenkavalier* to prove that he could have been just as successful had he wanted. He was probably the most unpopular composer of all time and critics have never liked the way in which he wrote for the orchestra better than most people. There are signs that Strauss will eventually become the most admired composer of all time when he has been forgiven his great success with *Till Eulenspiegel,* which manages to be both supremely clever *and* enjoyable.

Violent, emotional and vulgar are words which no longer need be used about Strauss. His most popular work is undoubtedly the first minute or so of *Also sprach Zarathustra.*

Stravinsky

set out to write music that would not be likeable in any way. Purged of all expressions of human emotion, it was simply to be a logical system of sounds. Through the long years he got more and more fustrated by his failure to achieve this peculiar ambition and, to his apparent horror, even saw some of his early works like *Petrouchka* and *Firebird* become immensely popular and spoken of with true affection by nice old ladies.

Driven to extremes by this manifestation of devotion on the part of the public he ended up writing works employing the **twelve-tone** method, often of about one and threequarter minutes duration, which were so mean and nasty that even some of his greatest admirers have been unable to encore them more than half a dozen times.

Not only has he become beloved but he has had a greater influence on 20th century music than any other composer. His disciples have written music that was even more off-putting than his own, and have thriven on it.

Mellowing somewhat in his eighties, he went round the world conducting and recording his own works so superlatively that one got the impression that even he grew to like them. Accompanied by a faithful Boswell called Robert Craft, he made pointed utterances which were all recorded by this Mr. Craft and published in book form. A very good thing for Mr. Craft.

Of course, Stravinsky was always making utterances. He once said that jazz was a 'subversive chaos of sound' and then wrote *The Rite of Spring*. Following that he wrote a number of pieces based on jazz and ragtime. A remarkably clever man.

Tchaikovsky

was born too early to write for films and thus missed a great opportunity to be rich and successful. His music, with its rich melodic vein, brilliant orchestral colour and strong emotional expression showed early signs of becoming immensely popular. Tchaikovsky became increasingly depressed about this knowing that he would never be taken seriously as a result.

You must not take Tchaikovsky seriously. He was once married for eleven weeks but quickly saw the flaws in it and the much better arrangement of living at the expense of a wealthy widow was adopted. He died from drinking unboiled water.

It is absolutely essential with Tchaikovsky to find some out-of-the-way work which never has had and is never likely to enjoy the popularity of his best symphonies and ballets and the *1812 Overture*.

Suggested unpopular works: Grand sonata in G; Concert fantasy for piano; and *Hamlet* overture. The first three symphonies are also interestingly dull.

Tippett

Although Sir Michael's music is very demanding and rarified, and the words (which he writes himself) equally so, there was no justification at all for the use of the phrase 'tippett and run' by one music critic left bereft of anything else to say. That sort of thing is not even worthy of a Bluffer's Guide . . .

Vivaldi

according to one unfriendly critic, spent his life writing the same concerto five hundred times. This was a malicious exaggeration – he only wrote four hundred and fifty (and he often took the trouble to change the solo instrument).

Additionally he wrote over forty operas, now rarely heard; which might of course be the same opera under forty different titles. Even his leading supporter described them as 'written in haste and confusion and full of waste material'.

One of his *Four Seasons* has been very successful. A carefully cultivated admiration for Vivaldi can be a great asset and who is going to question a casual reference to P.275 or P.374 – or any of the other four-hundred-and-forty-eight for that matter?

In a book of this scope it would be impossible to dissect every composer and everybody will find that we have left out just the very one that we should most certainly have included.

The aim of good bluffers, anyway, should be to find one composer that nobody else knows anything about and have a really superficial knowledge of him. An obvious name that comes to mind is Reger (pronounced 'ray-gar'), whose music is so unapproachable that it is difficult even to persuade critics to write about him. What better barren pastures to explore?

MODERN MUSIC

Modern music is that which is written in an idiom that came just after the period that any given music-lover was last able to understand.

To some, modern music still begins with Schoenberg (*q.v*) but to others Schoenberg is now as old-hat as Wagner or Delius. The point where music achieves the kind of obscurity and difficulty to qualify for modernity is infinitely movable. We have heard Berg's *Violin Concerto* openly described as 'romantic'. On the other hand people have been known to have listened to a programme of Webern and remained unaware that they were in the presence of music.

You may personally dislike modern music. If you are a normal sort of person it is very likely. Even most of the critics who make a living out of writing about modern music secretly play Mozart and Schubert for their personal pleasure. It is, however, blatantly foolish to declare your dislike openly as you can then gain no intellectual advantage over someone who smartly steps in and claims to like it.

You must cultivate terms like 'thematic structure', 'contemporary sensibility', and 'basic shape' and use them completely at random. Find a few special words of your own like 'paradigm', 'diplogical' and 'concatenate' (dip into a book on modern music for these) but remember not to drink alcohol while using them.

It would be impossible for anyone to be prepared for every contingency in modern music discussion. You can always murmur 'interesting' or 'ingenious' or, better still, make indeterminate noises. Never admit that anyone mentioned is actually 'avant-garde' but suggest that you are one step ahead by saying 'yes, but perhaps a little narrow in outlook' or 'rigid' or even 'predictable'. These are all terms which are difficult to refute.

Matters have been confused of late by the discovery that not all modern music is deplorable. There are still composers, like the Swede Eduard Tubin and the Brit George Lloyd, who write music which, if not quite of Mozartian delectability, is at least quite pleasant to listen to. The public were surprised and the critics horrified, the latter resorting to the word 'derivative' at every possible occasion. They were made much happier by the German Alfred Schnittke, who writes good old-fashioned modern music that sounds as if three works, all difficult, are being played at the same time. Schnittke was soon hailed as a leading composer and is played almost daily on the 3rd programme.

Just in case you are up against an intellectual it is dangerous to say, for instance, that so-and-so derives from Stockhausen as this may be questioned and then where would you be? Better to phrase it more ambiguously as 'going on from where Stockhausen left off' as nobody is likely to know exactly where that was.

It will entail a little work and use of memory but you should have a few basic words at the ready for use in connection with some of the prominent avant-garde. For Stockhausen, for example, 'isomorphic', for John Cage, well, 'isomorphic' would be all right there as well.

The best line of defence in modern music is definitely attack. 'How can one generalise' you might say, 'are we to assume some correlation between Babbitt, Musgrave, Maxwell Davies and Harrison Birtwistle?' Smiling, of course, so that it can be taken as a joke of some kind. Or other.

At this point it is best to say: 'But your glass is empty. Pray let me refill it for you.'

A FEW MUSICAL BYWAYS

Musical slumming is a very fine game and can be played with immediate skill by the most unseasoned of bluffers. All you need do is to take some fairly simple, commonplace music which has neither very much in its favour nor very much against it and, by constant innuendo, sly mentions and knowing looks, make people believe that you have found something that they have been unobservant enough to miss. Various breeds of music have become minor art forms through having this technique applied. If the subject can be wrapped in nostalgia – like old music-hall songs or songs of the 'twenties, then you have an easy task before you. Some kinds of music already well-established as cultural byways are:

Music Hall Songs

which were turned out in their hundreds by early Tin Pan Alleyites. Max Beerbohm and other creditable writers have given the stamp of their approval to the songs of broad and earthy humour that now make very good party listening for overwrought intellectuals, e.g.

a) Ted Sniveller singing *Never choose your wife from a photograph – it doesn't show round the back*
b) the way Hetta Tiller used to lead the audience in *There's a look in your eye that attracts me* (*if only, my dear, you had two*)
c) or Harry Winner belting out *Will you take this wedded woman to be your lawful wife?*

A little light reading amongst such authorities as Scott, Macqueen-Pope, Willson Disher and Chance Newton will quickly get you into the lingo.

You can do yourself no harm at all (as was once the case) by discussing the merits of Dan Leno or Marie Lloyd who have both been written about by people like T.S. Eliot. The great thing about music-hall and its music is that it is sociologically significant and is now the subject of earnest books and university studies.

Folk Music

The richest field for the musical slummer is undoubtedly folk-music; in its strictest sense, music that no-one can be accused of having written. The surest badge of guarantee is the word 'traditional'. This really confers the mark of mystery. A mere 'anon' simply implies that whoever wrote the piece was thoroughly ashamed of himself.

The whole thing goes so far back and is so totally undocumented that anyone can take uninformed guesses at its origins. Progress is so minimal that the addition of a single thought or note can take 10,000 years. Folk-music in the beginning was simply a series of unintelligible choruses which fellows used to sing together following a drinking session. The leading caveman would say: 'Now, all together lads' and they would burst into the refrain: 'With a humph-humph-grunt-grunt-willy-nilly-pooh' and then all roll about laughing and have another drink.

By the 15th century or so these choruses had advanced as far as 'With a fol-do-rol-de-diddle-diddle-dol' or the more sophisticated 'hey-nonny-no' type of thing. It was the same throughout the world with national variations. While the 'hey-nonny-no' was catching on in England, it was 'with a heigh-ho, heigh-ho, barney heigho' in Ireland, 'avec un trala, la a lère' in France: even in distant China they were at it – 'ming, ting, pitti sing, ting'; and so on.

After a thousand years or so this got a bit tedious. It was then that some spark, slightly brighter than the rest, had the idea for verses to link the 'fol-de-riddle-os'. He suggested 'As I went out one May morning' – which was then misrembered, misquoted and improvised on through an alcoholic haze up and down the country. Hence the interesting Gloucestershire and Shropshire variants discovered by Mr. Kidson in 1879 (a real conversation stopper).

This sort of thing went on for years until choruses went out of fashion, and the verse became the thing. The folk-song now became a long, elaborate and totally fictitious story on the lines of 'The good Sir Belvedere rode out upon his milk-white charger'. They were always going out – very few people ever came in.

By the 18th century the news of the day was being written down in ballad form and sold on ill-printed sheets of cheap paper some of which have survived other functions and become valued collectors' items. A name to remember is John Playford whose little book of tunes called *The Dancing Master,* and others like it became the source of folk-songs and dances ever after.

In the 20th century the learned interest in folk-music really began. It was then that the aforementioned Mr. Kidson, and the even better known Mr. Cecil Sharp started to go round with notebooks and, occasionally, recording machines, to capture and print these old folk-songs while there were still people around who could remember them and sing them in the proper tuneless sort of way.

You could always tell (and still can) genuine folk-singers by the way that they cup one ear in a hand and sing through their noses, thus leaving their mouths free for the passage of alcohol.

Light Music

Those who are only acquainted with serious music-making and are rather put off by some of the names so far bandied in this book, need not fear being left out of musical conversations altogether, however diffident they may be. Allow your opponents to dilate on the subject, and when they ask 'and who is your favourite composer?' say, quite firmly 'Albert W. Ketelbey'. While they are still reeling from this you add 'Born in Birmingham and studied under Prout. Do you know his piano sonata? A great favourite of Elgar's. His orchestral music shows a great flair for tone colour, don't you think?' It can hardly fail, and all you will have to do is swot up a few insignificant snippets from *The Oxford Companion to Popular Music*.

If Ketelbey (very popular in Japan and east of Suez) is not to your taste then you might try Leonard Bernstein; *Candide,* one of the best candidates for neglected masterpieces; Sullivan as a serious composer; the lighter side of Havergal Brian.

The likes of Johann Strauss, Franz Lehar and other Viennese masters, many of whose works sound identically the same, have already become well-established cults. The Kurt Weill campaign still has some wind left in it particularly now that his music has been recorded on the most modern equipment so that it sounds exactly as if it was recorded very cheaply in Berlin in 1937. A considerable technical achievement.

Such lowbrow sophisticates as George Gershwin, Jerome Kern, Cole Porter, Richard Rodgers and Irving Berlin may have been a little overworked; but if you are quick you might make a good line out of Maceo Pinkard, J. Fred Coots, Sammy Stept (one of the Odessa Stepts), Naceo Herb Brown or W. Benton Overstreet. All very neglected composers at the moment – and all genuine.

Jazz

is the modern heir to folkery. It all started in an obscure way at an unspecified time in American history and hundreds of books have been written confusing the issue.

There are two kinds of jazz:

1) Traditional, where they all play together and try to outdo each other, and
2) Modern, where each player goes on as if unaware of the existence of the others.

You must decide which you support and decry the other on every occasion; or if you can't make up your mind what you like say you prefer 'Mainstream'.

Jazz musicians no longer smile or look at all pleased when they play – a sure sign that jazz is growing up. After all, nobody would expect a symphony orchestra to look as if it were enjoying itself. The keynote of your approach to jazz should be deadly serious, the deadlier the better, and, as ever, the language must be carefully chosen. Nobody in jazz will misunderstand you if you say the opposite of what you mean. For instance, if you come across a particularly intellectual piece of jazz that might have been written by Schoenberg in a relaxed moment you could describe it as 'crazy'. The proper word for a really good piece of jazz that meets with your approval is 'bad'.

If anyone asks you who you consider the most 'under-rated' jazzman (a favourite adjective, this) you might say Dink Johnson. Or if they ask you who you consider the greatest of all jazzmen you could earn quite a reputation by nominating Eddie Condon. They just won't know what to say. The Beethoven of jazz is Charlie Parker.

GLOSSARY

To talk about music one need not swallow a musical dictionary, but it is obvious that some terms must be used which lie well outside the vocabulary of the common man. There are a handful of words which it is absolutely essential to have some vague understanding of – generally the difficult ones that need a lot of explaining.

Do not be discouraged. Below is a list of useful terms defined by their implications rather than their strict meanings which is the correct bluffer's way to use them.

Absolute – Music which does not suggest the sound of the sea or leaves rustling in the breeze, thus leaving the mind a delicious blank and prey to the enjoyment of pure sound. Hence 'absolutely divine', 'absolutely awful', etc.

Accent – Playing a Viennese piece in 3/4 time so that it goes da-dum-dum instead of dum-da-da. Foreign conductors have very strong accents while the British play B.B.C. style.

Accidental – A different note played on purpose.

Accompaniment – Conflicting points of view as seen by (a) soloists who deem it an obtrusive background to be kept at a low level; and (b) by accompanists who see it as a good piece of music ruined by the soloist.

Antiphonal – The music that results when half the choir has been given the wrong score.

Arrangement – An agreement between orchestra and conductor. They will behave if he will stop messing about.

Atonal – Music written when a composer forgets, or perhaps never knew, what key he was supposed to be writing in.

Augmented – Additional personnel added to a dance band so that it can play *The Blue Danube,* or to a symphony orchestra so that it can play Mahler.

Bel Canto – The lost art of singing properly.

Bowing – What all string players do wrongly, hence the phrase 'bowing and scraping'.

BWV (D, K, L, P, etc.) – Mystic code-letters given to the work of composers who have written so much that the old Op. number is considered inadequate. The letters stand for the names of the well-meaning scholars who did all the hard work. Vivaldi = P = Marc Pincherle; Scarlatti = L = Alessandro Longo; Mozart = K = Ludwig Koechel; Schubert = D = Otto Erich Deutsch; J. S. Bach = BWV = 'Barmy' Willi Vogel.

Cadenza – An over-long and unnecessary solo spot in a concerto which would have been obsolete long ago if the Musician's Union did not insist on them.

Chamber-music – Music written for a very small number of listeners.

Chromatic – Thick-textured music, implicitly romantic, with more notes than can be absorbed by any one person at any one time.

Classical – The word should never be used in the common way to mean music that needs listening to. It has the precise meaning of music of that period of pristine purity up to about Mozart and pre-tuba.

Coda – An extra bit at the end of a composition during which people can find their coats and put their shoes on.

Coloratura – When a singer, usually of unnaturally high voice, does more than is strictly necessary.

Concerto – The favourite music of impresarios. The only difference between a symphony and a concerto is that a concerto has an additional player known as the soloist. This makes for an interesting battle, giving both the orchestra and the conductor two adversaries instead of one – rather like a musical tag-wrestling match. With the help of cadenzas (*q.v.*) the soloist is usually the winner. At the end the conductor should graciously concede defeat and shake hands.

Continuo – A noise like a blue-bottle in a jam-jar, usually made on a harpsichord, which fills up the gaps in baroque music.

Contrapuntal – Music with two or three tunes all going on at the same time. Clever music.

Cor anglais – French reaction to Elgar.

Development – What composers do with the melody in order to produce a composition worthy of a fee.

Diatonic – Music that begins and ends in the same key with only brief and apologetic departures from it. Much better to refer to a composer's 'diatonic leanings' than to say his music is pleasant.

Discord – An obsolete term not in current use.

Double-stopping – See *Violinists*.

Dynamics – Playing too soft or too loud.

Enharmonic – The capacity to tell the difference between C♯ and D♭ – see *Violinists*.

Exposition – The popular bit of a composition while the tune is still being played.

Fingering – The mystique of playing an instrument that critics know nothing about.

Folk-song – Music on which, because the original composer foolishly preferred to remain anonymous, anyone can claim the royalties – if he is quick enough.

Fugue – Clever music generally played by organists.

Glee – Impresario's state of mind on a Beethoven night.

Grace notes – Notes thrown in for good measure.

Grove's – the 20-volumed Bible of the music-world. Realising the importance of this work to the student of music, most reputable building societies are now prepared to consider a mortgage; providing you can offer the security of a Strad or something of similar value.

Harmony – A term of no meaning whatsoever. Such phrases as 'rich harmony', 'stark harmony', 'satisfying harmony' can be used indiscriminately.

Harmonics – The buzzing sound that string instruments make – see *Violinists*.

Impressionism – Music that sounds as if it is being played in a thick fog.

Impromptu – A carefully worked-out composition.

Improvisation – A natural accomplishment amongst jazz musicians, but now only used in classical spheres when the music falls off the stand.

Interval – The pause between one piece of music and the next.

Key – Essential information to have if music is to be discussed with any degree of know-how – e.g. the G♯ minor concerto is much better than saying, 'You know – the one with the bit that sounds like *God Save the Queen.*'

Leitmotiv – A piece of music played every time someone makes an appearance in an opera. A good example can be found in *The Vagabond King*.

Lieder – Songs which do not have a memorable melody – see *Schubert*.

Madrigal – Medieval barber-shop songs generally sung out of doors on wet summer evenings.

Major – Keys which sound all right.

Melody – A word which, like tune, should not be used. 'Melodic line' is permissible but better to refer more vaguely to the 'thematic material'.

Minor – Keys which sound a bit odd.

Mode – Scales which sound a bit odd.

Modulation – The art of moving from one key to another in a manner that is subtle yet obvious enough to arouse admiration.

Motiv – A tiny and irritating tune used *ad nauseam*.

Obbligato – An accompanying part which, as the name does not suggest, is slightly unnecessary.

Opus – A code-name for a composition, the familiar use of which raises the status of the speaker 100 per cent.

Ornament – Notes used to fill in the blanks in early classical music left because the composers always wrote in such a hurry.

Ornamentation – The art of making early and baroque music more interesting (or, more tedious) by the addition of trills, shakes, turns, and so on.

Pentatonic – Music that can be played on bagpipes.

Perfect interval – A period of time long enough to queue up for, purchase, and consume, a cup of coffee.

Perfect pitch – The assumed possession of a sensitive ear that gives one the right to say that performers are out of tune.

Portamento – The ability to move from a wrong note to the right one without anyone noticing the original mistake.

Programme music – Music that suggests nice things to think about while it is going on – very popular with the unmusical and therefore included in as many programmes as possible.

Recitative – When an opera composer has lots of dull words to set to music and admits defeat.

Rhythm – The elemental musical sense which critics find most lacking in conductors.

Romantic – Music with themes suitable for use as background to films.

Rubato – Playing in an old-fashioned and blatantly emotional way. The less apparent a musician's rubato is, the more one admires it.

Score – (a) Complete copy of the music being played that all the best soloists and conductors like to do without; (b) Complete copy of the music being played that bluffer members of the audience like to have.

Sonata form – Rather complicated formal pattern for the first movements of symphonies painstakingly established by the early composers and studiously avoided thereafter.

Song – A *lied* with a melody.

Stopping – Technical term used by string players for fingering. Hence the expression, in regard to a violinist, 'not knowing where to stop'.

Subject – Trendy term for tune.

Symphony – A piece of music for many performers, played instead of a Concerto when the promoter can't run to the expense of a soloist.

Tonality – Trendy term for key.

Twelve-tone music – See under and after Schoenberg.

Vibrato – The minutely wavering quality of voice or instrumental sound that critics say most performers have too much of.

Voluntary – A piece of make-weight music that organists offer to throw in for no extra fee.

THE AUTHOR

Hailed as an infant prodigy, Peter Gammond was playing the gramophone at the age of three, revealing a natural winding action that was the admiration of all who beheld it. A well-known amateur through his years at school, in the army and at university, in 1952 he was at last persuaded to turn professional and joined a major record company.

Today, looking much younger than he seems, he is acknowledged as one of the country's leading gramophone-players, equally at home in the various fields of popular music as he is in the classical world, and now as tasteful an executant in the electronic age as he was in in the days of the 78. He also plays the piano, golf, tennis and fruit-machines.

He is the author of an excessive number of books on music. Most of them, as in the case of the present volume, have been compiled from the bits that zealous editors removed from earlier ones. Thus there is a remarkable uniformity about his work that many critics have eagerly noted. Most of all they provide a glimpse into the mind of a frustrated composer. Not many people know that he has written almost as many songs as he has books.

His wide non-musical interests include Indian curries, Evelyn Waugh, real ale, Offenbach, class-warfare and Things. He lives in a ramshackle house in Middlesex with a fine view over a row of garages and an old-people's home. A contented recluse, he is known to few beyond the immediate circle of his doctor, lawyer, accountant, golfing friends, listeners to the radio and a handful of devoted readers.

THE BLUFFER'S GUIDES®

Available at £1.99 and (new titles* £2.50) each:

Accountancy	Maths
Advertising	Modern Art
Antiques	Motoring
Archaeology	Music
Astrology & Fortune Telling	The Occult
Ballet	Opera
Bird Watching	Paris
Bluffing	Philosophy
British Class	Photography
Chess	Poetry
Champagne*	P.R.
The Classics	Public Speaking
Computers	Publishing
Consultancy	Racing
Cricket	Rugby
Doctoring	Secretaries
The European Community	Seduction
Finance	Sex
The Flight Deck	Skiing*
Golf	Small Business*
The Green Bluffer's Guide	Teaching
Japan	Theatre
Jazz	University
Journalism	Weather Forecasting
Literature	Whisky
Management	Wine
Marketing	World Affairs

These books are available at your local bookshop or newsagent, or
can be ordered direct. Prices and availability are subject to change
without notice. Just tick the titles you require and send a cheque or
postal order for the value of the book, and add for postage & packing:

UK including BFPO — £1.00 per order
OVERSEAS including EIRE – £2.00 per order

Ravette Books, P O Box 11, Falmouth, Cornwall TR10 9EN.